"In these dark times, the poems in Margaret Randall's *Wild Card* stoke the light of the imagination and stir the embers of social justice. As a poet and essayist, Randall has always called out to our better selves, reminding us of our responsibilities to one another. And yet there's an iridescence to this volume, written in Randall's eighties, that comes from layers of life being distilled and compressed. These are poems that nourish the soul and the ear: a long cool drink from Margaret Randall's deep well of wisdom, telling the age-old story of the power of art for the good—how 'imagination is [our] wild card' as human beings, our gift and our responsibility. A stunning achievement by one of the great poets of our time."

— Minrose Gwin, author of *The Queen of Palmyra* and *Beautiful Dreamers*

"Margaret Randall is ever sensitive to the distant roar, the body in the world, the movement of words across a line. These expansive and bold poems weave personal and communal witness, and confront us to attention in our increasingly dark world."

— Kenny Fries, author of *In the Province of the Gods*

"Here are Margaret Randall's keenest, sharpest words yet. All poetry creates something from nothing; Randall, however, transforms 'from absence to awe,' her global journeys winding here, to this book, just when we need it most—before she imagines the next thing, and the next, leaving us with this moment in her life's work to nourish us and inspire us."

— Zach Hively, author of *Owl Poems* and *Desert Apocrypha*

Wild Card

Selected works by Margaret Randall

Poems:
This Honest Land
Home
Time's Language II: Selected Poems 2019-2023
Time's Language: Selected Poems 1959-2018
Vertigo of Risk
Stormclouds Like Unkept Promises
Out of Violence into Poetry
Starfish on a Beach: The Pandemic Poems
As If the Empty Chair / Como si la silla vacía
The Rhizome as a Field of Broken Bones
About Little Charlie Lindbergh
The Morning After: Poems & Prose in a Post-Truth World

Nonfiction:
Letters from the Edge
Last Words
Luck
Artists in My Life
Thinking about Thinking
I Never Left Home: Poet, Feminist, Revolutionary
My Life in 100 Objects
Che on My Mind
Haydée Santamaría: She Led by Transgression
Exporting Revolution: Cuba's Global Solidarity

Wild Card

poems

Margaret Randall

Casa Urraca Press
A B I Q U I Ú

Cover artwork by Barbara Byers.
Author photograph by Sandra Stevenson.
Set in Nobel and Odile.

28 27 26 25   1 2 3 4 5 6 7

First edition

ISBN 978-1-956375-40-4

CASA URRACA PRESS

an imprint of Casa Urraca, Ltd.
PO Box 1119
Abiquiú, New Mexico 87510
casaurracapress.com

For Barbara

Contents

"Talent is insignificant…. Beyond talent lie all the usual words: discipline, love, luck, but most of all, endurance."

—*James Baldwin*

"A woman…
believes that if she speaks, she might break apart,
the dust of her flying across stooped men
chained by their debt to the fields. She presses both lips
together, an effort to hold her own grief in her skin."

—*Karenne Wood*

"You know you can't explain everything…. There's this critical analytical mind … and that's rational. But then there's also a kind of itch you keep wanting to scratch."

—*Elizabeth Diller*

Reflection

I stand before the mirror.
From the other side
of the glass, the terrorized face
of a young girl
stares back at me.

Her eyes have witnessed a world
I have never seen.
They are dulled by brutality,
emptied by the loss
of those she loved.

Behind her, the devastation of Gaza
stretches in endless rubble.
Some still scream for help
while others have gone silent
in death.

I turn away in shame.
When I look back,
Charlie Chaplin is working hard
to make me laugh.
Harriet Tubman struggles to her feet.

Mine is a benevolent mirror,
not the addictive landscape
cocaine users bend over to snort a line.
It hangs on my wall,
eager to give me what I need.

I have spent years searching
its reflecting pool,
anxious to discover myself,
to find my own image
in its mystery.

Just now, I finally see
the weathered face
I recognize as mine, my years
etched in mottled flesh
breathing deep relief.

Leave Nothing Behind

Waking, I make sure
I bring every piece
of myself into my day,
leave nothing behind, trapped
in some fanciful dream, lured
by the promise of a better life.

So many years have left me
careless and at risk
of losing an idea or body part
to that shadowy world of night
when sun has escaped
my window.

I know what I leave behind
won't be there
when I return to sleep
the following night, nor
will I find it beneath my bed,
cleverly swept out of sight.

I am careful to keep myself
together: tiniest bone
and brash decision, weary muscle
or new idea born at the edge
of a vivid dream's ominous swamp
and left to rot.

Even a partial memory, clothed
in secrecy and subterfuge
must not be left in that land
of sleep. You never know
when it may bloom
in the light of day

and allow you to access places
you've forgotten,
where you will build
a house of many rooms,
large enough for every
descendant to live.

The Rules Have Changed

I was born with the sound
of English in my mouth,
so read our story left to right
picking up bursts of light
along the way.

Traveling this narrow trail,
sheer drops on either side,
I glimpse others running
to keep up or fleeing the energy
of my feet.

Along the way, I gather bits
of Brooklyn bravado,
a passion for poetry,
high notes of resistance
and a tropical lilt.

I play with irony, keep fear
deep in my throat,
dress my words in kindness
when and where there is room
to breathe.

Adding Spanish to my repertoire
multiplied my power past
the horizon, because split tongues shine
when not crowding
a single mouth.

When both sides are yours, you confront
cries that attack your integrity.
The rules have changed
and you must defend your voice
with your life.

Here I Am

"The forest was shrinking but the trees kept voting
for the axe, for the axe was clever and convinced
the trees that because his handle was made of wood,
he was one of them."
—*Turkish Proverb.*

My right arm, sheared from my body,
fell down a cliff
of no return.
I tried to grab it with my left
but had to steady myself so I wouldn't
tumble after the appendage.

There goes the turquoise ring
you gave me. I wore it
every day of our love.
That broke my heart, but I knew
loss would be part
of this impending doom.

Hope was the gravity that kept us
moving toward a utopia
mirage-like in indecision.
I know I must steady myself,
not by conformity's poor ruin
but as an armature of resistance.

Disappointment in seventy million
of my countrypeople,
rage at their complicity
and disgust with that figure of hate,
the Pied Piper who would lead us
to the ovens.

I know I must put my grief and rage
aside, climb down
from this dangerous height of scorn,
and take my place among those
who understand the price of freedom
in a land that has sold its soul.

Here I am. Still willing. Mostly able.
Weathered but eager to share
what I've learned with those who
must assume the mantle of necessity.
Gravity is also the power of art
on a new horizon.

Listen

Listen carefully. You have heard
these drumrolls before.
Their echo adds decibels to fear
like a heart at journey's end.

Listen with your memory. Exercise
that muscle almost exhausted
by the cowardly assaults it suffers
in these times.

Listen to the muted whispers of those
who wouldn't be silenced
even when their reward for obedience
came with a prize of years.

The hoarse voices of ghosts
tell stories with knife-sharp edges
that dissipate the haze of forgetting
in this hazardous story.

You will hear their fighting sounds
in the language babies babble
before they must rein in their words
to meet our poor demands.

Listen for those messages twisting
and turning in your dreams,
syllables you will never decipher
when awake.

Listen. Pay attention. Do not let them
distort or erase what you know
to be true, what connects you to
your only life.

The Diary

Spent the night making documents, a dozen ration
cards and four passports. T will bring the stamp
tomorrow. Demand is great, and it's hard to keep up.
Last month ...

The rest of the sentence is gone,
torn away by the writer
or someone else.
Fear of entrusting words to paper
or the ravages of time?

Initials stand in for names.
The letter T appears
on almost every page.
Menace presses against my throat.

It rained yesterday and I couldn't complete the
deliveries. Warned T about S, who has been asking
questions.

Three pages later:
T has disappeared. His apartment is empty, but the
lights were on all night. When I asked the woman next
door, she said she didn't know ...

Not a proper diary with pages
assigned to days of the week
and months of the year,
but a simple notebook
called into duty
by necessity.

I don't know who kept
this diary,
found in a house
that has had many occupants.
It comes from another country,
a different time,
yet breathes like an avalanche
of warning.

Relegated to an attic
for decades,
it is a chance discovery
among old clothes, musty books
and other discards
that have outlived their use,
threatened by cobwebs,
rat feces and a leaky roof.

It conjures memories of a war
we no longer remember,
perhaps one that promised
to be the last,
then broke that promise
many times over
as if killing could bring peace,
wounds heal.

Dates too are entered by hand
but never a year,
only the number of a day,
the name of a month.
I know I will never find
every piece of the puzzle,
never be able to write
an ending that satisfies.

*10 January. Today we lost R. Someone saw her marched
with others to one of those trains without windows,
transports headed nowhere ...*

This page exudes a warning,
pressure compresses
my lungs, hovers on my lips,
making speech impossible.

Beside the diary, a small cigar box
holds photographs,
ordinary snapshots of ordinary people,
none older than thirty
yet no children,
no one smiles.

A man stands on a bridge,
an ornate public building
behind him in fading light.
A young couple holds hands
in a city park.
Two women on a bench:
sisters or lovers.

The erasure of memory returns us
to where we were,
stranded in an endless spiral
that can only lead
to grieving repetition.

I close the diary, return the photos
to their box,
then go out and buy
a notebook, spread its resilient spine
with trembling hands
and begin to write:

*27 January 2025. G and R received the letter. Someone
slipped it under their door last night. We have
organized message drops ...*

The Village Clock

The village clock, tired of telling time,
calls out my secrets instead
and I'm left vainly trying
to protect their fragile boundaries.

This morning, a secret I thought safe
sounded on the quarter hour,
causing a million accusing eyes
to turn and stare me down.

Like our anthem's bombs bursting in air,
twenty dissonant chimes an hour
then one each minute
outpace what I've labored to forget:

cold nights of terror and false patriotism
reenacting their sibling rivalry,
impossible to achieve a peaceful settlement
as they pummel my flesh.

Neither my mother's winter coat
nor a bouquet of white roses
can negotiate my safe return
from this journey clinging to my bones.

In the Words

If we reference biblical prophecy
rather than human compassion,
will settler colonialism
pass for neighborly enclaves?

If we choose the term *victim*
not *aggressor*,
can we justify the murder
of sixteen thousand children?

If we remember the holocaust
without also remembering
that survivors become perpetrators
when revenge overpowers pain,

and call it *righteous*
instead of *genocide*,
will the goat herder of Ramallah
ever sing to his flock again?

Choice Is Never Easy

Help when none is needed
turns distress inside out.
Now you must care
for the one who means to care
for you.

We didn't get here by accident,
you say, *we chose these hills*
running out to desert expanse,
its cacti displaying needles
along with their flowering fruit.

Choice is never easy, invitations
are too often double exposures
where now is superimposed
on before, an overlay
that hurts your eyes.

We come into this world hungry
for our first taste of air,
our cry a sign of survival.
We may die alone, but memory
has tender arms.

Help when we need it responds
to the fearless invitation,
the one we don't think about
although it takes every bit
of courage we can muster.

Failure to Read the Fine Print

Without warning, time disappears,
taking language with it,
leaving you looking for breadcrumbs
or some other sign you can follow.

Just as suddenly, it may reappear
wearing an arctic wrap
on the hottest day
in recorded history.

Warning you is a responsibility
I inherit from a long line
of female ancestors,
every one of them silenced by secrets,

bolstered by broken promises, perennially
on sale at your neighborhood
convenience store, five for ninety-nine cents
on national holidays.

I believed time stronger, more resilient,
surely more honest in its readiness
to help us color outside the lines,
step on every sidewalk crack.

I'd failed to read the fine print: *To make
this element work for you, you must
sign here and initial every paragraph twice
before the age of three.*

Default

As long as man's default
is conquest,
young girls climb a ladder of terror
hoping for a horizon
of stars
and small nations fly flags
in primary colors.

As long as the goal is profit
above care,
the sick get sicker
in this country
where magical machines
can map the human body
inside out.

As long we breathe
the toxic air
of forever waste,
our lungs will shrink
and *wake up and smell the coffee*
will become an arcane proverb,
its meaning lost to time.

Memory is the last to go,
its default mode
that long journey to a place
without context.
Millennia of progress
promised better
until we failed ourselves.

October

Arriving at the shoulder of the year
in hand-me-down clothing
brings a chill to the air,
the scent of piñon smoke and signposts
like devious messages.

For me, it is the month I gave birth
to my first child, a great heart
replacing loneliness, the time of year
when all rivers empty to the sea
leaving behind their polished stones.

Later there was that revolution
that sparked broad hope
before it showed its breakage and regret:
an aging sofa with torn upholstery,
sagging springs.

For you, the month brings memories
of people who weren't what they
claimed to be, images that pursue
your nights, terrorize your days
and leave you undone.

A single month, showing us
both sides of humanity,
telling us power always has two faces
and it's up to each of us:
plead guilty or reclaim yourself.

Her Failures

The poet asks herself
how she got here,
what magnet pulled her
to this point on a map
that migrates with her years.

Some days she counts
each failure
woven into the blanket
she clutched to her heart
as a child.

Some days she bows
to inspiration
as if it were a visitor
from outer space:
unexpected, alien.

She cannot stop.
Other artists
remind her
she hasn't that many
years left.

But she ignores such warnings
growing like weeds
in this garden
where the healthiest flowers
succumb to neglect.

Maybe her failures
have something
to tell her—like lessons
that stumble just
as she opens the door

to welcome them in
from the cold.
Maybe she should study
their language,
learn to inhabit their fear.

From Absence to Awe

Time closes its eyes and takes
a quiet moment for itself,
exhausted by the demands
I place on it.

It claims I have treated it
like a child
incapable of understanding
adult solutions.

It whispers it would give me
so much more of itself
if only I would trust it
to lead the way.

This poem, for example,
needed time to look
deep inside itself, understand
how it came from nothing

and faltered, stumbled,
picked itself up
to inhabit the confidence
it now exudes.

Convoluted journeys make
unexpected stops
along the way,
gather chance encounters

and nourish sudden questions,
risky offers
that must be considered
honestly.

The magic of art resides
in its journey
from absence to awe:
a lifetime in the making.

Troubadour

Antonio Castro, 1940-2022

You came, slight of frame,
intense,
with your powerful song
and Venezuelan cuatro,
like a small guitar
of breathless accompaniment.

You weren't Venezuelan
but Colombian,
your desperate family
breaching the Andes
and losing your younger brother
to hunger along the way.

Later you endured poverty,
struggle and prison,
before an island called Hope
took you in,
became your safe harbor
in treacherous times.

And we shared a piece
of those times,
joining our voices
in brief parenthesis,
a map destined
to fray and fade.

Now, two years too late,
I learn of your death
in some distant land
where questions
outnumber answers
ten to one.

You abandoned your silhouette:
modern-day troubadour,
maker of music
and poetry
in a world that still needs
your voice.

Among the Debris
of Homeless Wisdom

John Nichols, 1940-2023

The story we heard was that he died
writing, but the truth is
he was in his armchair watching TV
with a glass of eggnog, half full

or half empty, depending on
your point of view.
I decided to go with the better story,
the more exciting fit, and so I say:

His heart stopped as he sat at his desk
doing what he'd always done:
writer of books,
polemicist for light.

And I wonder if he'd completed
the word at his fingertips
or a bit remained in a mind
hurrying to get where no one wants to go.

If a fragment trembles in a world
gone dark, will it be found
one day among the debris
of homeless wisdom crying for help?

We all say we want to depart
doing what we love,
but interruption always enters a plea
that carries a penalty—

if not for the protagonist,
for his hungry audience.

Lost Cathedral

Try on a tone of voice for half a day.
Let it mark the sky
in slow bolts interrupted,
the whole body of it shaking down the alley
or flying like a kite
lifting blue landscapes
into the stratosphere.
No astronaut or cosmonaut has mentioned
hearing that tone of voice in space.
The wet earth staggers through the door
with clouded hat in hand.
The ghosts of younger silhouettes
still chase the empty room
filling it with tension
and exhalations of music.
Listen! Sing! Mutter the notes in your soup.
A chorus of events echoing
from canyon wall to cosmic calcium.
A scrim of green lightning chases
the orange fissure and our last words
rise quietly in the morning sky.
When my words deserted me,
were they following ancient latitudes
or haunting my tomorrow?
Where are they now?
Don't answer unless you know for sure.
Words ache to grow among the sagebrush
and salmon berries, shout to make off
with the best strains of daylight.
You close your eyes
and the sky grows thin wings.
They take me home.

Cedar Sigo and Margaret Randall
September 11, 2024

Slithering Through Dimensions

Poets walk differently now.
It's the in-between matter that works as mortar.
They are applauded for their hesitance
or random screeds between poems.
A handful of sharp straw and spit,
a dropped note like *never the same river twice.*

Where we're born also matters.
Umbilical cords buried in fresh earth,
magnets anchoring them,
calling them home.

Slither through dimensions,
don't succumb to being left out,
mumbling the tempers of a defunct music.
Our histories will be gathered
from yellowed fragments, drowned recordings,
joyous readings in chorus.

In the end we miss the poets themselves,
in their bodies,
how they sounded skirting certain words,
talking with friends, calming a nervousness,
circling the page before sifting
for workable parts.

In the Amazon insects burrow in flesh,
lay their eggs, reproduce beneath the skin.
We must burn them out to keep
on speaking, hold our own:
my grief and my resistance,
my willingness to cross the sea again
and take notes that form
the line of our sailing.

The language was jealous of the water,
a common distortion
when elements are kept separate.
Time bends to the shape of our lips.

Cedar Sigo and Margaret Randall
September, Friday the 13th, 2024

Difference, Once Intriguing, Even Revered

In sixth grade I learned about Henry David Thoreau,
his devotion to nature
and how he sat by Walden Pond:
endless inspiration
for his philosophy of life.

I was older when Harriet Tubman and Sojourner Truth
entered my consciousness,
the first given to sudden fits of narcolepsy,
the second a woman who bared her breasts
to make her point.

Albert Einstein didn't speak until he was four,
then went on to revolutionize physics,
quarreled with a government
that believed
splitting the atom heroic.

And then there is Leonardo da Vinci:
curiosity unleashed, inventor
of dreams and artist who painted
that side of life
we cannot see.

Taught to admire alike the quiet philosopher,
soldiers for justice and odd little boys
who were geniuses,
difference wasn't to be feared
but something that enriched our lives.

Today we are threatened by those unhoused
men and woman who amble too close
to where we keep ourselves
safe from difference,
oblivious to need.

How many Thoreaus, Einsteins, Tubmans
or da Vincis wander among us,
walking our streets in search of a handout,
shelter, or someone interested
in what they have to say?

Difference, once intriguing, even revered,
frightens us now: a danger
that might seduce us away
from those bland answers to the questions
permitted by our rule of law.

Moonstone

Perfectly balanced on the shoulder
of this new year,
a knotted hope
holds its internal glow.

Like the moonstone covered in fresh snow
far to the north,
its light touches me in this southern world
that closes its mouth and waits.

The moonstone, smooth as an egg,
has been waiting breathless,
will continue to wait until
everyone has left the public square.

Then babies' first words will begin
to echo ancient rhythms,
their eyes closed against our alphabet of shame,
their lips forming new landscapes.

Will those places make sense to us?
Will we take the challenge
and weave a language
that lifts us above the flame?

Your Body's Memory

Use that wall as your canvas,
get right up in their faces.
The owners of the wall
will cry *private property*.
You are telling them
your imagination is your property
and they aren't just getting
in your face
but crawling inside your head.

Reach back to before your birth.
Unearth the people
and their sorrows, the places
and their darkest seasons,
all that finds direction in you.
Write from where the wires
short-circuit in your ears,
eyes, mouth. These are the words
that set you free.

Move your body with abandon
as if no one ever used it
against your will,
no one told you how to dress it
or to pretend it helpless
to boost their ego.
No one left it out in the cold
to tremble in shame
or die before its time.

These are the gifts you can give
those placed in your care,
those who ask questions
and look to you for clues
or consume what you paint,
write, sing, dance.
Your body's memory
moving through space.
This is the gift you give.

Art and Money

When the elite auction house announces
bids will start at a million dollars
for Maurizio Cattelan's *Banana on a Wall*
I'm not surprised.
Art and money merge so easily.

Imagination and talent have no place
in this exchange. The banana
is held to a wall by gray duct tape.
Are we to consider it serious art
or a hoax to attract the one who has everything?

If I mention the Guatemalan workers
who haul heavy boughs of fruit
through fields owned by Chiquita,
Del Monte or Dole, this poem will be
called propaganda.

If I question calling it art, I will be named
a traditionalist, incapable of moving
with the times, stubborn in my insistence
a line has been crossed
in our understanding of art.

Before the auction house, iterations were sold
for $150,000 as if they were prints
in a run produced on a lithographer's stone.
One was eaten by a hungry student
who failed to consider its subjective worth.

Who do I blame for this travesty? The artist
exploiting a world that supports
such sham? The gallery claiming its value?
Or the buyer who can think of nothing
else to do with his fortune?

And when the banana blackens and rots
as all picked fruit must,
will the million dollars have been spent
on a fanciful moment or will it become
a tax-deductible loss?

Like the fall of Rome, we are swimming
in a sea rank with the stench
produced by those of us who think
only of ourselves, the pollution we ignore
at future's peril.

* When *Banana on a Wall* by Italian artist Maurizio
Cattelan (1960) went up for auction at Sotheby's in
2024, the bids outpaced expectations, and it sold for
$6.2 million.

A World Where Perception Rules

Secrets can live forever, withstand
extreme heat and vicious cold,
aren't prone to childhood accidents
or the serious illnesses that end
so many lives.

When still an infant, I noticed
a fearful one lurking
behind a curtain, no way of knowing
what it meant
or that it would follow me.

Later I learned we can birth
our own secrets,
some with clean hands
and masks
they wear and remove at will.

Still later, while traveling my map's
precipitous trails, I understood
we must banish all secrets
to permanent exile,
even those promising delight.

If you're lonely without your secrets
consider this: there is nothing
so beautiful as the clear gaze
of one who tells the truth
in a world where perception rules.

Just a Housewife

Just a housewife, the phrase
tossed out to disparage
women's work: ordinary
as it is repetitive,
worth nothing at all.

We know it's worth nothing
because no money
changes chapped and bleeding
hands, no raise
to be expected.

Men in business suits
select a tie
that speaks of taste and power.
They give no thought
to the chef who followed

that complex recipe to their
avid taste buds,
made their bed and cleaned
the place they call home, raised
these children who do them honor?

My name is Housewife.
I applied for the job
with the best resume,
most impeccable qualifications,
eager to please.

You hired me with promises you knew
you'd break, gestures of love
turned bitter in memory,
all the while shaping me
to your whims.

Now that I have left you
to seek another job,
I place my memory shards
in a chest of freed hopes
and tell you

I am as proud of my Housewife
title as I am of Poet or Maker
of New Things.
My children and theirs
carry the imprint of my love.

I know a light touch
at the stove is art
just as the poem
shaped by risk and imagination
speaks my name.

A woman after all, I'm paid
for neither profession
but the commendations in self-worth
would be enough
for me to do it all again.

My Map

For Greg Smith and Rich Gabriel

I venture onto the map my memory offers up,
its shifting elevations taking my feet
to places that feel new
even as old images emerge from shadow.

Land features and human construction
hold their ongoing dialogue,
a poet's call and response
in a language sharpened by desire.

Symmetry and asymmetry compete
for the same space
illuminated by hues
that change second by second.

Bursts of light form color
and shape,
presenting me with new stories
even at this late date.

No one who accompanied my years
speaks in a rhythm I understand
but I am listening now
for wind and silence as they search

for safety and comfort while honoring
a landscape that embraces
what we impose upon it
in our arrogance.

My map asks me to go slowly,
savor moments lost
the first time here.
I am transported to an era

before the digital highway
made everything too easy,
erasing those narrow trails
that sang awake my youth.

When the time comes, I know I will
be able to shed my skin,
lay down on a sun-bleached rock
and re-enter the dream begun so long ago.

My Okavango Streams

I try to remember when *be careful*
gave way to *you can do it*
and who first uttered those words
that would guide me from then on.

Was it Miss Peak, my third-grade teacher
who praised the vines and buds
I drew in the margins
of my simple paragraphs?

Was it Elaine, who smiled when I said
I'd rather try my hand at drawing
than model nude for her
painting class?

She bought me a fifty-dollar brush, said
Beginners need the best.
Her advice was *Try it all* and I followed her
to New York to do just that.

Nancy? Alfred? Ruth?
Laurette and all the others
who modeled risk?

Like great rivers whose tributaries feed
smaller streams,
then trickle into creeks where they
continue to nourish thirsty land,
wise voices fed me what I needed
to become the woman I am,
and I feed those
who need what I can give.

If we could view this map from above,
it would resemble the Okavango Delta,
its glistening ribbons twisting and turning
as they seek receptive soil.

And just as the Okavango recedes and dries
in seasons of want,
waterways of inspiration
will fade and disappear
when humans stop caring
about passing it on.

Our creative resources live
only when multiplied in those to come:
poets, painters, makers of music,
cooks and tenders of gardens,
healers who see the whole person,
not just a single organ or surface rash
in fifteen minutes of corporate consultation.

The key is to offer more,
then stand back
and let those we feed
measure our offering
according to their need.

We give less than what we have
at our sad peril.

Today I honor the rivers and streams
that nourished me:
born and sought, old and young,
women and men,
those who looked me in the eye
and those I read about in books
who gave me wisdom or courage.

Without you, I wouldn't have
risked risk.
I'd be a poet today
but not the one I am.

And I extend my arms, mind,
time and energy
to those who look to me for food.
I still contemplate
my offsprings' journeys,
a grandchild's question,
delight in a great-grandchild's drawing,
careful not to ask her what it is.

When to say more, when less,
when nothing at all:
these are the dilemmas
I ponder every day,
will until my time is up
and the river branches out
seeking other directions
across this wondrous map.

My Shadow's Silence

She wakes in form, ready
to witness the events
of the day
even if not destined
for an active role.

But the sun is relentless
in its path
and she cringes and shrinks
as she recoils
clear of its power trip.

By noon, she finds herself reduced
to the minimum expression
of herself.
I hold my breath, fearing
she may never breathe again

for I admit she comforts me
in times of uncertainty,
adds to my stature
when I feel small
or cannot find my voice.

My shadow, tethered
to a point of no return,
travels that mysterious line
from dawn to dusk
escaping death every single day.

I know she cannot speak for me
—what would a shadow say?—
but sometimes she's my only listener:
patient and willing
at my side.

Never the Devil's Advocate

Say enough but not too much.
Be kind but never present
the other cheek.

Move over but not out of sight.
Dim the lights
but search the shadows.

Remember what can help
you live,
but not what kills.

Speak up but listen to those
whose voices
were throttled.

Make the first move or last,
but model dignity
as you go.

Never the devil's advocate,
only mapmaker,
poet, gardener:

stitching your small corner
of the world
back together.

Organ Recital

More often than not, when I ask
how an old friend is doing
the response is a litany
of ailments and despair.

The doctor limited to fifteen minutes
per patient, not enough time
for a complete list of new symptoms
accrued since their last visit.

Activities no longer possible,
trips not taken,
long list of daily medications
and their rising costs.

Description of an operation
in gross detail
causes eyes to glaze over
and attention to waver

until all conversation wanes and
we bid each other goodnight,
wondering if weather or food
might not be a topic

better suited to make
our next visit
one that promises
the possibility of future.

Our Hair

Legend tells women to braid our hair.
The din of modern living
obscures the message for some
while others heed its sage advice,
twisting their long strands
closely together,
eliminating all space between.

The prescription works for any
culture or tradition:
Afro, corn rows, pink and green dye,
ironed silky straight or forced
into nightly torture devices
that bring on the headaches we bear
in beauty's name.

We are told tight braids will trap sorrow,
not allow it to enter our eyes
and make us cry, that they will take
the poison from our lips
so we don't speak bitter words.
Braids urge us to conform to those
who always have the final say.

It must be true. How else explain
the silence she balances?
Just as we no longer
need imagine
the old woman who has lost
her luxuriant tresses
in any but her current dignity.

And just as we know the woman
who shaves her head
plays coyote to every male hope
and female submission
with a newfound freedom,
laughing retort,
an image no one can decipher.

My Breasts, Encore

Flaccid but far from done,
nostalgic duo
drawing into themselves
secreting memories of breathless hands
and powerful infant lips
sucking immunization and health
from standup nipples.

It's been a while since they've been
willing to imprison themselves
in a bra, useless to try to tease them
into cleavage now,
those days are gone.
But if breasts could speak
mine would have stories to tell!

Solidarity runs through ducts
where milk once flowed.
They remember adolescent angst
pushing themselves up and out
beneath the matching sweater set
at a high school dance
or awkward first date.

My breasts know harder stories too
about other women
forced to smother their babies
when hiding from an enemy,
fearing the betrayal
of a child's cry
might give them all away

and how that impossible choice
belongs to a history
embedded in skin
that separates body parts
too often applauded frivolously
from the pain
of a beating heart.

Sometimes at night I caress mine,
their velvet flesh
grateful for long years
of companionship
in a world where a woman's body
must defy convention to survive.

Risk

For Mary Oishi

My first was the deep red velvet gown
snubbing its nose at all the girls
in delicate pastels:
baby blue, pale pink, white purity.

In high school, defying a female
culture of submission
was like signing the warrant
destined to destroy success.

Later my risks were more daring
though still games:
climbing a wall at midnight to swim naked
in a motel pool, driving a pickup truck

of old tires out a dirt road to deposit them
in an ancient volcanic crater,
setting them on fire and retreating
into thirty years of conspiratorial silence.

Risk took on serious meaning
when I birthed my first child
husbandless and defiant, then put my life
at the service of justice for all beings.

Now, in my final years of life, risk is
simply a fondly remembered friend.
We don't see each other much anymore
but I wake with a smile when I've dreamt of her.

Remembering Pompeii

Oh yes, I remember it well:
Mount Vesuvius
towering over the ruins:
imposing reminder of nature's power
to devastate.

I knew I was in for wonder,
I'd seen photos,
even paintings of the place:
revered by lovers of natural beauty
and sudden calamity.

Coming upon the first body
caught in the act of dying,
imagining that instant:
escape impossible and fate
claiming its terrible prize.

Between the horror of death
and ordinary gesture:
a raised spoon denied waiting lips,
legs trying to run
with nowhere to go,

I forced myself to shift my gaze
from those bodies
to the faded majesty
of mosaic walls and floors,
art as relief and balm.

Except here's the thing:
I've never been
to Pompeii or Herculaneum,
never experienced
those sites myself.

And yet, memory tells me its story
undeterred by time or place
but it's another's memory,
lifting mine to a place
it doesn't know.

Do I blame my memory
for the false positive
or revel in all the times
it's been
my unfailing guide?

Rumbling Toward Eruption

A volcano rumbling toward eruption,
the poem powers to its birth.
Along the way its magma flow
retrieves a secret whispered generations back.
Its searing heat carries traces of women
discarded through millennia
and small surprises of courage.

A gentle breeze from the south tries
to cool its fury. Genocide
masquerades as righteousness,
throwing obstacles in its way. Lava streams
must choose direction and purpose
as they cleave the land, each offering possibility
or an opportunity missed.

I let them take me where they will
but no shortcut
can replace those nights
when an idea or silence enters my dreams
or bolts me upright, demanding I rise
from warm blankets and my lover's body
to record a word against forgetting's threat.

My final challenge is to scramble from its path,
give in to voices resonant in memory
and get out of the way.
This half tango, half duel
settles for nothing less than victory
in its dance to the finish.

Smile

Does it arrive spontaneously,
unexpected response
filling a face with joy?

Or is it a mask, mannered rictus
encouraged by polite society
learned and mimicked thoughtlessly?

Let this gesture of genuine delight
claim its small place
in our sorrowing world,

evidence we may still revel
in those moments
that tell us who we are.

Reading Scripture as History

Armageddon: last battle between good and evil
preceding a metaphorical Day of Judgment
according to those who read scripture
as history. Or perhaps just
an archaeological site on the plain of Esdraelon
south of present-day Haifa
in the state of Israel.

We scoff at a fairy tale that chains enslaved minds
to dogma designed to take curiosity
from its beautiful play
yet disregard the Armageddon we construct
with our constant violence,
senseless wars, injustice
and rape of future.

Consider the map. Observe the planes taking off
in that troubled place
carrying death and destruction
to a people
who could have been family
in a compassionate world.
It's only prophecy if we declare it so.

The Futile Act

Hurting inanimate objects
is a futile act, immune
to explanation or excuse.

Yet I have been guilty of it,
once destroying
a child's rocking chair,

the sweetest piece of furniture
among the requisitioned items
in our Havana apartment.

Enraged at the man I lived with,
I hurled it across the room
and witnessed it shatter against a wall,

relieving not even a little
of the angst I carried
in my woman's heart.

Hurting living beings
is worse:
not only useless, unforgivable.

Misplaced rage is like
trying to breathe
where there isn't any air.

I will carry that only time
I hit my child
to the end of my journey.

I do not seek her forgiveness
or forgive myself, but hope
my daughter thrives despite my crime.

The Good Marriage

A slippery see-saw, the marriage bond beckons
wearing one mask or another
from the time we are little girls.
At five or six we play: I'll be the husband
you the wife, gender irrelevant to the game.

Play turns to desperation in every social class:
the society hopeful paraded
before an assemblage of prospective husbands,
queens destined to marry other royals
to perpetuate monarchic blood,

while at life's other end a flirt,
broad hips, or cooking skills
seduce the attention of working men.
We sing to love but unless we fit
the acceptable world of either/or

we'll have to fight to marry the one
we desire or invent a cover
that satisfies those who won't acknowledge
its magical state
as reason enough to wed.

I do is the goal, even when those words
lose themselves among the rules
we endure and lies we tell ourselves,
rather than in those yearnings
we know are right.

The Promise Rosary

A rosary of promises intercepts
his smile, leading her
into a trap of subterfuge.

Like the gift of a glorious afterlife
his apologies evaporate
in real time.

The rippling effect attacks
her rocking chair
and every hopeful sunrise.

She believed the fairytale
long before they met.
A new story clamors

for her attention, but all her roses
wither beneath the weight
of those menacing thorns.

There is a quilt of history waiting
to be stitched together.
It would keep her warm

but she doesn't see it, untethered
as she is from time,
all maps indecipherable

and she finds the doors
camouflaged by signs
to places she fears to go.

It's too late for her, but maybe
her daughter
will make it home.

Their Animal Sensibilities

I watch the newsreel—men on horses
in Mississippi, 1964,
and wonder about the horses.
I know all I need to know about the men.
Did those horses know
who they were charging,
the crimes they helped commit?

Magnificent manes and sweat-coated bodies
glistening in the heat of unequal battle,
the stun of hoofs crushing everything in their path,
deceitful dance of legs and great weight
aimed at innocent prey,
even the depth of those millennial eyes
gives no clue.

We think we understand the animals we keep
but know little about those we use and abuse,
imagine they feel as we do
or assume they have no feelings at all.
In their animal sensibilities,
do they resent where we take them
and what we make them do?

The dogs who stormed South African townships
or lay at the feet of Goebbels, Hitler, Hess.
India's sacred cows
crowding traffic on New Delhi streets.
Elephants nurturing memory, and lions
whose parents roamed savannah
confined in zoos as we stroll past their stolen lives.

The crow who unzips your backpack surely
removes a bar of soap and hoards it
for reasons we can't understand.
Whales whose resonant language
we struggle to decipher.
House cats we imagine impervious
with their languid ways and expressions of disdain.

I have seen them all in pictures, on film,
or in the homes of their people,
even those who love them well,
and wonder what they think and feel,
if they know judgment,
have frustrations or regrets,
and if we will ever meet on common ground.

The Raw Material of Words

It might be the nudge of an idea
but often it's a single word
that appears to guide me
onto the map I create.

If it's *dewdrop* I immediately
discard it,
knowing there is no circumstance
in which it can succeed.

If *spirit*, *soul*, or *hearth*, I am wary.
Their intentions may be good
but cliché sounds a deafening warning
in my ears.

Traditional forms such as sonnets,
villanelles, rondels, or haiku
rarely attract my attention.
Cacophony rankles my senses.

Door is always a good beginning
because what's beyond
promises a challenge worthy
of poetic skill.

For opposite reasons, *wall*
is just as seductive,
inviting me to pierce
its obstinate membrane.

When numbers appear, they evoke
the kabbalah or calendric time.
Seven is mysterious,
seventeen a nonstarter.

Colors are just as tricky.
Red brings power
or violence into the poem,
green a pastoral conclusion.

Terms such as *capitalism* or *corruption*,
far removed
from music or rhythm,
are the hardest to juggle.

Memory embraces every word
shaped by my history,
imbuing it with the authenticity
I alone provide.

But it's the unexpected word
—for example, *ridicule*
or *fabulist*—that often visits
in the night, taunting mercilessly.

It will keep me awake, tickling
my consciousness
like a dream:
neither nightmare nor balm,

it won't give me rest
until I find a place
to keep it safe while my fingers
reach for the keys.

Dawn receives me then
with its map of trails
one leading to another
and the poem breaks free.

Where the Words Go

My old friend calls to tell me
she's losing words.
She opens her mouth
and silence uncurls before her
as she struggles to remember
what her mind refuses to release.
It's getting worse, she says.

Did those words give up,
exhausted after
too many seasons at play?
Are they stored in guarded vaults,
hidden in plain sight, or relegated
to cemeteries where we mourn
for their return?

I try to imagine the anguish
trapping a mouth
no longer able to obey
a mind still alive with ideas.
Thoughts frayed at the edges
yet beckoning still, calling,
taunting determination.

Language grows from childhood
to maturity,
and still there are things
it must learn—
how to get along with others
while its appetite explores
the coves of a dangerous shore.

For women, how to say no
and repeat that word
until all who need to hear it
do.
How to make our voices heard
above accusations of *angry*,
strident, *brash*.

For men, how to lower theirs
to a gentler register,
try humility on for size,
take a breath, or two,
instead of barging through
every door forced open
by their bulk.

Tongues, lips, throats working out
like gymnasts practicing routines
until mind and body
settle into perfect sync.
Strong teeth chewing on new syllables,
savoring the dance that matches
sound to meaning.

Older versions hibernate,
sleeping through
long and painful winters
recharging memory,
preparing for the important battles
while newly coined expressions
try to convince through novelty.

Slang, lies and the threatening secret
dance with moans, gasps,
laughter that oversteps its boundaries.
Forked tongue and witty retort
stretch the fabric
in directions that surprise
or delight.

The crisp talk of northern lands
or seductive song
in sultry temperatures
caresses the vocal cords.
Clicks, grunts, a movement
deep in the throat
or springing from animated lips.

Language births itself
in the child's mouth,
picks up speed
through the years
only to come to a sudden stop
for those unlucky enough
to have the gene.

The baby babbles a sound
only it understands.
A young poet wants to create
a new language to express what is,
while at life's far end
some struggle to hold onto
the words they have left.

It's all part of that single cry
last heard in a mythical
tower called Babel.
And for all whose power
shatters unity,
threatens community,
robs us of understanding.

The vicious enemy couldn't know
that difference translates
to riches in the mouths of those
who mine the depths of wonder
until language itself
grows weary of its vehicle
and leaves.

Where Words End

For Bob Arnold

Way back when, but that was before.
She was different then.
What she couldn't understand
is nowhere in memory.

A poet wrote a poem he called *Fucking*.
It says: *Going to the grocery store*
with the one you love
isn't going grocery shopping.

A poem written out of a relationship
that is itself a poem:
same texture of forever,
same silence where words end.

My Life as Alphabet

Now my feet are farther apart when I walk,
creating a broader base and claiming
more territory. This stoop I cannot right
has me hovering closer to the ground.
No longer the svelte L, I have become an A,
my legs reaching for balance, foundation
shrouded in socks that try to hide puffed ankles.

Puffed as in swollen, fluid retention
from one of the many pills I take
or maybe my remaining kidney, tired at last
from working alone these many years.
One resolution wrestles another
and may the best one win
if winning is even still the goal.

My back is half an M, not two humps
but one, like the dromedary
to Bactrian camel, and it stores
no nutrients, nothing I may claim
as advantage to these years
when change moves relentless
in only one direction.

My mission now is to cherish the A I am
and stop longing for the L I was,
sure every letter in the alphabet is needed
to write the language of a life
in symphony with other lives,
the time and space I must yet travel
on this journey to my rebellious but grateful end.

My Table

My table expands to embrace
the traveler who speaks
a language I do not understand
but comes in hunger.

Even if only water or bread,
I will always find
something to add to the pot of soup
simmering on my stove.

*Your seven-dollar donation will
make the difference between
fascism and democracy* is reminiscent
of *turn off the lights to save electricity,*

the burden always ours
while corporations deplete
those resources we have
with no regard for future.

Global warming affects us all
but logic demands
the responsibility for slowing it
be divided fairly.

War is savage, its perpetrators
pompous in their safety
while its victims rarely know
why they kill and are killed.

My table is a generous field
where good things grow
but I'll resist to the end
those clever words designed to shame.

Like Pieces of Words Too Tired
to Pick Up Their Feet

I woke with someone else's memory
in my head.
My dream had a different taste
but I didn't understand the full sweep
of difference until I swung my feet
onto the cold floor and realized I knew
nothing beyond my bedroom door.

Exploring this place where I lived
took well into afternoon.
The clothes in my closet
were two sizes too large
and I thought I hated lime green
but discovered shirts, scarves,
even underwear in that hue.

What confused me most
was my old memory
taunting me from around the corners
of the new—
like pieces of words
too tired to pick up their feet
and run.

The moment I knew the challenge
might be too great
was when I began to sense a blocked few years
of my childhood
hovering just beneath the surface—
after all the work it took to unearth
what I forgot first time around.

Now I wonder who has my memory.
Does it roam in someone else's head
or is it dispensed to a realm
where everything is forgotten
and empty faces
wish for even the most horrific image
as proof they are alive?

Lime Green

Your favorite color was lime green,
perhaps still is:
sweaters and scarves like flags
adorning your slender body,
strong from years of yoga and running.

I love you but hate lime green,
always taste the hue
as bile or baby poop.
Other greens evoke nature to me
but not that nauseous shade.

I was a mature adult when I discovered
the experience of matching colors
to words, faces, ideas,
has a name and isn't something
everyone shares.

Colors as language, like numbers
or memory,
colors as landscape or code
singing their own praises,
impersonating only themselves.

Synesthesia dislodged me from a habitat
of kinship with my species,
one of the many marks of difference
we endure or enjoy—
and I eagerly searched for others.

Your preference for lime green
no longer rises in my throat
when we meet. I've learned to admire it
along with the other generous buds
that open in your garden every spring.

Tools

Now I celebrate those makers of tools,
not the inventors whose glory
won them laurels and prizes
but those who imagined how to fix
their inventions when they broke.

From flintstone, arrowhead, and fire
to hammer, mallet, and implements
as complex as the things they mend:
ideas applied to other ideas
by hands that care.

Not Franklin and his kite but he who
fashioned the meter
an electrician pulls from his toolbelt
to locate the broken connection
in our journey of light.

Not the jeweler who dreamed the circle
of gold that graces the ring finger
on my left hand but the one who crafted
the mandrel that stretches or contracts it
when age requires a new circumference.

Certainly not the likes of Elon Musk
who invents nothing of his own
but exploits worker bees to tackle the puzzles,
building their grotesque empires
of power and fortune.

The inventor who gave us common cans
lives in our history books
but what of the mind that imagined
the can opener without which
we cannot taste what's sealed inside?

Nations fight over whether Bell or Meucci
invented the telephone but no one thinks
of those who make the microscopic instruments
that keep cellphones ringing
in the palms of our hands.

Gutenberg comes to mind each time
we open a book, but every cleaner
of lead fonts keeps that magic alive
for all those minds hungry
for the adventure we call reading.

Clamps, screwdrivers—Phillips or flat—
brushes of every dimension, blades,
solvents, pastes, oils, soldering irons,
measures and weights, heat, cold, water
and the healing caress of human breath.

We admire the chimpanzee
and other animals
when we notice they wield tools to forage
and feed, rendering them more like humans
to our anthropocentric minds.

Who knows the name of the man
or woman who brought us
needle and thread, resin, glue, wrenches
that handle bolts of different sizes
and all those other tools that grace our days?

Lathes, papers coated with grains of sand
of differing weights to smooth
the rough spots on objects mistreated,
weathered or abandoned
in our lives replete with things.

Today the imagination that sees
how something works and,
unpraised, creates the tool that lets it
go on working, inspires the gasp
of wonder that is this poem.

This Inherited War

Women, taught from before we're born
to be ever vigilant, are alert
to every threat as we practice the words
designed to keep us safe.

Men, always ready to violate, invade,
and occupy, never stop
weaponizing the gift
of their twisted language.

Men who really do believe *no* means *yes*
simply speak louder,
imposing words charged
by conquest's deception.

While those who reject binary imposition
journey to their true identities
and must invent a new language
that speaks their name.

As poets, our job is to create a map
where words are comfortable
as old clothes, not too loose, not too snug,
and breathable as unpolluted air.

Speaking our truth is only half this war
we've inherited. The other
is getting a deceitful system to listen.
That's when peace may come.

When a Story Breaks Free

The nine-year-old falls silent
but his sock puppet
speaks of last night's shooting.
Its secret cuts through pummeling air
and becomes a trail.

When the fourteen-year-old whispers
so softly I struggle to hear:
That happened to me too...
what you said in your poem,
I knew the power of my voice.

In her sixties, my friend admits:
Those years we spent together
were hell.
She was speaking of the partner
she'd defended even to herself.

When a story breaks free
secrets lose their power,
breath returns, and a map,
drawn with invisible ink,
reveals itself.

Where Desire Turns to Stone

In my ninth decade, news
of a friend
is more likely than not the last:
one more goodbye.
Familiarity morphing to memory
as dear ones leave.

This morning Emma's molar
finally fell out,
her smile
a crooked grin.
The tooth fairy left a peso note
beneath her pillow.

My elders leave as my children become
parents, then grandparents
and I hover in the wings:
the great-grandmother marching
in this long parade
of beating hearts.

Eight-year-old Guille sounds out
the hard words, already plays
a cunning game of chess.
Little Julia at one, observant and decisive
in her cousin's arms,
claims her own safe place.

Immersed in such fortune, I ponder
the generations in Gaza
dying beneath the bombs
as others struggle through
the Darién Gap or Mediterranean waters
in search of life itself.

I would ask why some families
uncurl in joy
while others break
beneath this mania for violence
we have nurtured despite ourselves,
but my question disappears

into a chasm of pain
where desire turns to stone
in an error of judgment
no God could right
nor human call back
from danger's precipice.

With the Passion of Dreams

If our foreheads had windows—small porthole-like
openings blinking like the lens
on an old Leica—would we see a world
where the leaves of trees
change color with the passage of dreams?

Worlds within worlds don't guarantee us
deeper sight, bring a higher register
of sound or save us from the terrorist attack
we birth through gluttony, greed,
and endless swagger.

Only the poem's language, innocent and curious
on its calendar of ancient storms,
can stop this rampage of careless hate,
these landmarks that don't belong
on any map.

You Coped by Staying

Hettie Jones, 1934–2024

Death, in its finality, is always sad
although when pain or dementia
are involved, our grief
is tempered by relief.

If the departed was young
it's worse,
if very old we say:
at least it was
a long life.

But there are deaths that defy
all expectations,
refuse to obey the rules,
burden us
with unexpected sorrow.

I remember when you
told me I coped
by leaving, you by staying:
a poet's
turn of phrase.

Maybe if you hadn't still biked
the Lower East Side,
your four-foot-ten stature
weaving through traffic,
astonishing crowded streets.

Maybe if you hadn't been a white mother
of two Black daughters,
voice for justice, rebel warrior
at a time when sex
was all men wanted from us.

Maybe if you hadn't written
a memoir that tells it
like it is, taken the stairs
to your fourth-floor apartment
two at a time, grinned as you

talked about fighting a hotel to save
the place you called home,
showed me how
you got a running start
then leapt onto your high bed—

In my memory your big voice
still shouts the lines
of Ginsberg's "Howl"
decades after Gallery Six
and brings down the house again.

Permission

For Richard Vargas

We gonna send all you fuckers
back where you came from.
You don't belong here.
Hateful words
coming from a man behind
the dark-skinned mother and daughter
in the checkout line
while the cashier scans each item,
pretending not to hear.

This woman and her teenage daughter
are doing their weekly shopping
in the neighborhood
where they've brought years
of casseroles to deaths and births,
where the daughter walks
to school each day.

Trembling now, the girl makes
eye contact, starts to defend
her mother and herself.
The mother pulls at her arm,
urging silence.
The cashier is still ringing them up,
feigning innocence,
looking the other way.

A nation's people have been given
permission to spew the fear
and hatred in their hearts.
But we have never needed permission
to claim our space, fight for justice,
speak kindness and practice solidarity.

Which permission will travel
the greater distance,
reach its destination first,
is the question
we must answer now.

Promissory Note

I was born in 1936, a note pinned
to the umbilical cord
swimming behind my surprise.

The note congratulated me on my birth
to a comfortable white family
in this *greatest country on earth,*
as if I'd been given a choice.

It guaranteed perfect teeth, healthy genes,
and protection by the husband
I would win with seductions
honed throughout my youth:
all opportunities befitting my gender,
race, and family circumstance.

It assured me I'd have no cares as long
as I played by the rules
and didn't venture
beyond the walls.

Across an ocean, ominous boots
prepared to trample
a world I needn't think about.
Don't worry yourself was the message
etched in fake snow or bright lights
in every neighborhood window.

Just down the street, people
defective or *just plain lazy*
faced winter cold on stoops
and in dark alleys.
Better not give them money
they'll only spend on cheap wine.

I'd not yet found
my people.

My promissory note was written
in millennial code.
I couldn't erase it if I tried.

But the promise turned out to be
a deceptive holding pattern
where losing is made to look like winning
through lies and clever language,
the pounding of fists
in air turned toxic
with misplaced power.

When I gave birth to my children
I made sure
I'd battled such promises and won,

and not even an IOU remained
to clutter their journeys
through the places they would breathe
to life.

The Glass Has Gone Dark

Back then I couldn't see the map
or its torturous byways,
didn't imagine where they
would take me.
Life was anxiety: would he kiss me,
who would see, and what
would it feel like?
If I stayed at it, could I write
about something that mattered?

Mostly, could *I* matter, and how
to make sure I did?
Who knew about such things
and where were they hiding?
What would I become
and how could I get there.
No map, though,
just the wondering
in tandem with my anxious heart.

All these years later
I try to remember
who that young woman was,
the expectations
and how they burrowed beneath my skin,
at the closed end of a swallow
or in the eagerness
of budding breasts.
No one can tell me.

I search a granddaughter's
face, a grandson's poem,
my children's children
and the great-grandchildren
I've lived long enough
to cherish.
The glass that once reflected
both our worlds
has gone dark.

Double Exposure

Cold creeps into old bones
and settles—
stifling movement,
mocking a calendar
reading spring.

Your lips brush against mine
tender and warm,
welcoming me to another day
of what is still here
for us.

Weather is like this as we age:
it holds an image
of where we've been
superimposed
on where we are.

The Function of Words

Stan Persky, 1941-2024

Words seem to fail, struggle to reach
the heights or depths
of our experience,
and this is when we need them most.

We need them as signposts, pointing us
toward the fullness of feeling,
as shovels heaving emotion into view,
as legacy to help us remember.

Tears release this constriction
of heart muscle,
try to fill this empty space
I hold in my hands.

But words demand their place
on the stage of my grief,
have a job to do
and know it.

I have no words is the lazy way out,
uneven ground that threatens
to cave beneath our feet,
toppling us where we stand.

You left this battered world today
and I say your name,
dressed in words like memory, heart,
curiosity, pain

to describe how I feel about your death.
I will not say *he passed on*, pretending
there is another place and you
are there, not nowhere

but in the memories of those
who loved you as I did,
in all the words you left us
to evoke your name.

You chose yours carefully: gift
of your relentless journey
to discover who we are
behind the masks.

No, my words don't fail me today,
only battle with this loss
that tries to leave me mute
but can't.

The Photos

In the photo of my two-year-old self
bright eyes flirt with future.
Curiosity moves gesture, hands, feet
as I begin a journey that will make
of my map this place I own.

As years pass, I grow taller
and stronger, each limb
reaching for excellence. If a dancer,
my skeleton might have ascended
to positions of perfection,

if a scientist, the stoop of my shoulders
might tell of endless hours
bent over a microscope or notebooks
with meticulous records offering proof
of my contribution to the puzzle.

A mother who fed generations,
broad hips and eager hands
reveal marks of love's intention,
moving past exhaustion more days
and nights than memory records.

A poet, endless combinations of words
pulse soundlessly on wavelengths
unreadable on any photographic surface
or hologram that may be ordinary
in years to come.

In one small image I am spatchcocked
to the wall of toe and fingerholds
in a climbing gym, my body reaching back
to a strength I can barely call up
as I try the impossible.

In another, older now, I am on a podium
standing a foot from my hero,
a man larger than life
promising justice to a nation,
my hands blurred in applause.

And in yet another, I am with two
great women of words. By now
we know the energy of promise
is a garden we must tend
with the porous grief of every season.

As I age, the photos reflect sudden
or subtle changes: thinned hair,
weathered skin, thickening ankles,
the pulse of arthritic fingers
once chubby and tentative,

then steady, capable, or clumsy
in their longing to do
what they once managed with ease.
Features regress, almost disappearing
into pale silhouettes of themselves

until, nearing the end of my journey
along this arc of my only life,
I can no longer find that young girl
who took the world in her arms
and made it hers.

Witnessing a series of images passing
at twenty-four frames per second,
I try to record my life's dance:
its longing and energy dying out
as it nears its imminent end.

Free to Say I'm Done

There are only two bequests
we can hope to give our children.
One of these is roots, the other wings.

In Spanish they call it *dando a luz*,
giving light:
the act itself illumination,
a child meant
to brighten the world.

My first changed everything,
cleaved me in two
complete beings,
the newcomer I hoped would
continue my genes, will, ideas.

The second divided time and energy,
a mathematical calculation
destined to help me discover
a new radius of love,
another infinite number.

The third brought mystery, a quiet
garden where flowers
never seen before
blossom in winter
then turn to perennial seed.

The fourth traveled language
to inhabit another country,
leaps hurdles
like the fastest runner
in a race not yet run.

And I discovered difference,
how beauty walks
in many shapes and yearnings,
asking us to watch and learn
as humans become themselves.

In my children's children I still see
glimmers of myself,
trace a love of struggle in one,
a map of words or insatiable need
to offer food in another.

Now those children are giving birth
to children of their own
and I search the shape of a mouth
or movement of hands
looking for something I can own.

There is no startling hologram,
no straight line or easy road,
but a powerful web in bloom
that leaves me free
to say I'm done, and go.

Holding onto My Life

I'm holding onto my life, running across
uneven land,
this end of the kite string wrapped
securely about my wrist.

Above, swaying in a gentle breeze,
tissue paper colors—blue-green
with fine black stripes
and flecks of blood red
reflect sunlight and risk.

Those colors call my name, drawing
a map of the world
for me to follow to journey's end
braving shadows
that murmur *Look our way.*

I must continue running to keep
my kite flying,
cannot stop even when exhaustion
overcomes me and I am alone
on a field of obstacles.

An armature of ideas I share
with my people
keeps me going.
Community supports
those dancing colors
flying out of sight above.

I release more string, giving
my tether buoyancy
and hopeful lift.
I am almost flying now
despite complaining feet.

Close to invisible, my kite
is a tiny speck
against endless blue,
barely a reminder I was here,
gave it my all, spoke.

Let Us Call on Memory for Help

*"More and more, I'm beginning to think that the true
mark of assimilation in America is forgetting."*
—Lisa Yin Zhang

Sometimes danger requires
we resist
for ourselves and for those
who can't.

Sometimes it asks us to hide
silent, unnoticed
until the perfect moment
for attack.

Be alert in the four directions:
east, west, north, south.
Danger wears many masks,
speaks in many tongues.

It may be dressed as scripture
or a triumphant flag,
appear as teacher, protector
or friendly fire.

The lion's growl, bear's claws
or ominous rows of teeth
in a shark's mouth
are only looking for a meal.

Humans kill and maim
out of nothing but greed
or the lust for absolute power
over others.

Smile alone, or shout so you're heard
on every continent
depending on where you are
when the axe is about to fall.

But beware: danger's devious
weapon is making us fear
everything and everyone.
Let us call on memory for help.

You May Search for Preamble

*"I felt I was creating reality itself,
and that my reality was a better world."*
　　　　　　　　　　　—Danny Lyon

At some point in your life
you may search for
preamble, someone whose genes
are linked to yours:
heroic evidence or sad conformity.

She might have been a quiet seamstress
who sewed hidden pockets
into the linings of dirndl skirts:
transporting bullets
to people fighting the good fight.

Or a brash actor who drank
himself to death
after performing the perfect Hamlet,
leaving behind seven children
who hated theater.

You hope you won't find a rapist,
con man, or wealthy entrepreneur
who made his millions
exploiting workers
forced to live one day to the next.

Nor do you want submissive women
pretending contentment
at the whim of those who brutalize them
in the name of an invented God,
father of us all.

It would be satisfying to unearth
a great-granddad who painted
uniquely powerful canvases
destroyed in the San Francisco earthquake
and fire of 1906.

Or his daughter who wrote the music
her deaf ears imagined,
unheard by a world that believed
no genius could exist
in a realm they couldn't know.

You may overlook an unmarried aunt
who kept to herself,
lived a life of make-believe
buoyed by patience of the sort
you've always lacked.

The set of her eyes and nervous
gesture of her hands
a prologue to your own.
She moved determined, confident
despite the silences.

You see her frozen in time,
hers, not this one,
her mouth slightly crooked like yours
and awkward as she uncovers
secrets before they come due.

Hers is the truth that would
set you free
if only you knew how to read
the signs, pierce the code
she carried to her grave.

Perhaps, looking for heroism
you will find someone
who fought on the wrong side
of a necessary war, his face
in the photo curiously proud.

But think of your own descendants,
a century from now.
Searching their history, they may
stumble upon your name, catch a glimpse
of your face or read this poem.

Imagine that person wanting to know
about the things you made or did,
if you changed reality,
what you could possibly have to do
with them.

The Story That Is

Searching for balance, we run
away from ourselves,
look for that black hole
beyond which oblivion beckons.
We are hoping to stumble
upon the portal
in Alice's looking glass.

They have set the world on fire,
they who are slippery, hard
to grab and hold onto
even when screaming in your face
and laughing at the horrors
they fashion from lies
dressed in shining armor.

Stop. Wait. We are running
in the wrong direction,
cheated by devotional masks,
nightmares posing as rest stops
along a highway
going nowhere
at the speed of light.

They coax us to leave ourselves
when we must turn inward,
rediscover compassion in a memory
almost deafened by their shouts,
caress our lovers' skin, tongue
the salt lick in that hidden valley
they say we cannot enter.

We who don't know war on our shores,
aren't forced to hide from the bombs
or bury our children in the rubble,
we who only hang by our thumbs
metaphorically:
It is up to us to tell the story
that is.

Breathing Memory

Sight and hearing claim places
of honor in our sensory life
but olfactory memory
assaults me now, by turn
seductive and vile.

The pungent odor of burnt plush
rising from the backseat
of a 1940s Ford still accompanies
news of Pearl Harbor
as I try to calm my parents' fear.

In damp forests a decaying whiff
of mushrooms warns me
stay alert, my rigid body marking
distance in all directions,
terror invading every orifice.

And that unmistakable warning
hovers anywhere.
Subtle or strong, I breathe it
when no one else
can smell its presence.

From any battlefield, the stench
of rotting flesh screams death
in my lungs today, just as it did
when we moved those long-ago bodies
from their makeshift graves.

If you have ever known the odor
of decomposing humans
you won't forget
its tragic message of finality
and loss.

The reek of shame destroys,
rage does too.
They make us tremble
in the night, keeping us
from ourselves.

The scent of Old Spice or tobacco
my father tamped into the bowl
of his briarwood pipe fills my nostrils
with his gentle presence
all these decades past his death.

I bury my nose in the remnants
of the shirt a dear friend
gave me sixty years ago
and her wisdom-powered voice
returns a thousand-fold.

Today I fill our home with the aroma
of bread, rising and baking,
fresh from the oven
and filled with promises
both savory and sweet.

Like the comforting essence
of your body beside mine
in the bed we share, it is
the delight that banishes all others
and holds me to my years.

We Have Been Here Before

I will look for solace in a song,
a poem, a painting,
feel for it along the contour
of your body,
move toward it in dance,
search for it on the farthest horizon
and listen for it in old stories.

I will pay attention to silence too
as it rises from the lips
of those not yet born and is
bequeathed us by those now gone
who looked to us in their mirrors of hope.
All those who nurture life
must dance together now.

I will savor solace in the primal flavors
of winter stews
and summer fruits,
nurture it in the scent
of homemade bread
kneaded with an energy
born of patience and rage.

And I will do my part,
add my small thread
to the vast quilt of life,
patching its worn or faltering squares
as I make my way
through the wasteland
ahead.

We have been here before.

Wild Card

I walk the red rock canyons
of my desert
accompanied by footsteps
and the whispered voices
of those who walked before:
our legacy of time.

Their stories begin with need:
the search for water,
where to find the best hunting grounds,
calm hunger, build shelter
from heat and cold,
as they teach the young ones.

Over millennia, they change
in form and content, vary
in intensity, are told in different voices
and adopt surprising twists:
a bit of humor, sudden surprise,
endings rhythmic as the seasons.

Their stories imagine the unknown,
calm pain, undo death,
explain what causes storms
and what they mean,
why sun warms the earth
and night follows day.

Sometimes the whispers are shouts
or a pulsing agony.
Excitement dances in the air
crackling like electricity
in my ears,
jolting me awake.

Curiosity punctuates this
communal memory,
the heavy breathing of dreams,
an unexpected blow to the gut.
Mystery laced with hunger
and braided with secrets.

Sweet secret's evil twin, threat,
is its sibling's opposite
and with its innocent sister
begins a sinister journey
in search of
the most vulnerable.

Divisions rise between those
who revel in dependability
and those whose difference
inspires fear or jealousy.
Mistaken loyalties dig in their heels,
bringing religion and unending war.

Imagination is the wild card,
the unexpected element.
From the moment it emerged in
the history of human development,
how it bloomed in us
enhancing every culture.

Imagination: what brings us art,
makes us human,
the only thing that can save us
from banality
and despair
when the ordinary is spent.

About Me, Know That

with age I have more to say but also value silence.
Memory is my best legacy.
As our surround becomes more sinister, I nurture
the light thousands have brought to
        this journey.
I hate secrets but love surprises.
I intuit the mind/body connection and still search
for its pathways on every map.
Risk is my middle name.
I will look directly into your eyes and tell you what
I think.
I invite you to do the same.
Discovery, like invention, is a gift.
Imagination is the drumbeat of possibility.
Change encourages us to do more, be more.
I am as proud of each of my children as if I had
given birth to their brilliance.
My grandchildren, great-grandchildren and those
descendants I won't live to know
        carry my heartbeat and my song.
Like Brecht, I know: *In the dark times there will be
singing; it will be singing about the
dark times.*
And art is where I live.

Margaret Randall (b. New York, 1936) is a poet, essayist, oral historian, translator, photographer, and social activist. She is the author of more than two hundred books. She lived in Latin America for twenty-three years (in Mexico, Cuba, and Nicaragua). From 1962 to 1969, she and Mexican poet Sergio Mondragón co-edited *El Corno Emplumado / The Plumed Horn*, a bilingual literary quarterly that published some of the best new literature and art of the sixties.

When she came home in 1984, the government ordered her deported because it found some of her writing to be "against the good order and happiness of the United States." With the support of many writers and others, she won her case and her citizenship was restored in 1989.

Randall's recent titles include poetry, essays, and other creative nonfiction. These include her 2020 memoir *I Never Left Home: Poet, Feminist, Revolutionary* (Duke University Press) and two volumes of selected poems called *Time's Language* (Wings Press).

Her most recent projects have been two books based on her correspondence with people she calls outriders, creatives who have faced serious obstacles but have pushed through them to make and do. *Letters from the Edge* has been published by New Village Press, with *More Letters from the Edge* forthcoming.

Many of Randall's titles have appeared in Spanish translation from Siglo XXI, Alforja, Ediciones de Medianoche, and Heredad in Mexico; Casa de las Américas, Ediciones Matanzas, and Vigía in Cuba; Abisinia and Tinta Limón in Argentina, Rumbo in Uruguay, and independent publishers in Nicaragua, Brazil, Ecuador, Peru, Colombia, Venezuela, Spain, Holland, Japan, Turkey, and India.

Randall also translates from the Spanish. She has produced English-language poetry collections by Roberto Fernández Retamar, Roque Dalton, Otto-René Castillo, Carlos María Gutiérrez, Daisy Zamora, Kelly Martínez, Israel Domínguez, Alfredo Zaldívar, Laura Ruíz, Chely Lima, Rita Valdivia, Reynaldo García Blanco, Yanira Marimón, and Gaudencio Rodríguez Santana, among others; novels by Freddy Prestol Castillo, Juan Antonio Hernández, and Tomás Modesto Galán; memoirs by Gregory Randall, Lurgio Gavilán Sánchez, and Stefano Varese; and anthologies of Cuban poetry and short stories, Ecuadorean poetry, US poets for Mexico, and Beat Poets in Spanish. She has read her own work and delivered keynote addresses in hundreds of venues throughout the United States, Latin America, and other countries.

Two of Randall's photographs are in the Capitol Art Collection in Santa Fe. In 1960 Randall was a recipient of a Carnegie Fund for Writers Aid Grant and a grant from the American Academy of Arts and Letters revolving fund for writers in need. In 1989 she was a co-winner of the Mencken Award, and in 1990 she received a Lillian Hellman and Dashiell Hammett grant for writers victimized by political repression. The Barbara Deming Money for Women Award was given to her in 1997, and in 2004 she received the PEN New Mexico Dorothy Doyle Lifetime Achievement Award for Writing and Human Rights Activism. Randall received the 2017 Medalla al Mérito Literario, awarded by Literatura en el Bravo in Ciudad Juárez, Mexico. In 2018 she was awarded the Poet of Two Hemispheres prize by Poesía en Paralelo Cero in Quito, Ecuador. In 2019 she was awarded an honorary doctorate of letters from the University of New Mexico, and in 2020 she received the George Garrett Award from the Association of Writers & Writing Programs (AWP) and the Paulo Freire Award from Chapman University. She received the City of Albuquerque's Creative Bravo Award in 2022.

Randall lives in Albuquerque with her partner (now wife) of more than thirty-nine years, the painter Barbara Byers, and travels extensively to read, lecture, and teach.

Casa Urraca Press

Casa Urraca Press publishes creative nonfiction, poetry, fiction, and other works by authors we believe in. New Mexico and the US Southwest are rich in creative and literary talent, and the rest of the world deserves to experience our perspectives. So we champion books that belong in the conversation—books with the power, compassion, and variety to bring very different people closer together.

We are proudly centered in the high desert somewhere near Abiquiú, New Mexico. Visit us online to read more from our authors, browse all editions of our books, and register for writing workshops at casaurracapress.com.